LEVERS

IN MY
MAKERSPACE

by Tim Miller and
Rebecca Sjonger

CRABTREE
Publishing Company
www.crabtreebooks.com

For the guys who keep everything running behind the scenes at MAHC:
Rick, Mark, Larry, Murray, Randy, Brett, John, Ron, and Harold

Authors: Tim Miller, Rebecca Sjonger

Series research and development:
Reagan Miller

Editorial director: Kathy Middleton

Editor: Janine Deschenes

Design: Margaret Amy Salter

Proofreader: Petrice Custance

Photo research: Margaret Amy Salter

Production coordinator and prepress technician:
Margaret Amy Salter

Print coordinator: Margaret Amy Salter

Photographs:

Shutterstock: © Kisov Boris p13 (right inset);
© dmitrieval p21 (right); © javarman p25

Craig Culliford: pp8-9

All other images by Shutterstock

Library and Archives Canada Cataloguing in Publication

Miller, Tim, 1973-, author
 Levers in my makerspace / Tim Miller, Rebecca Sjonger.

(Simple machines in my makerspace)
Includes index.
Issued in print and electronic formats.
ISBN 978-0-7787-3371-3 (hardcover).--
ISBN 978-0-7787-3377-5 (softcover).--
ISBN 978-1-4271-1901-8 (HTML)

 1. Levers--Juvenile literature. 2. Makerspaces--Juvenile literature.
I. Sjonger, Rebecca, author II. Title.

TJ147.M562 2017   j621.8   C2016-907411-0
                                         C2016-907412-9

Library of Congress Cataloging-in-Publication Data

Names: Miller, Tim, 1973- author. | Sjonger, Rebecca, author.
Title: Levers in my makerspace / Tim Miller and Rebecca Sjonger.
Description: New York, New York : Crabtree Publishing, [2017] |
  Series: Simple machines in my makerspace | Audience: Ages 8-11. |
  Audience: Grades 4 to 6. | Includes index.
Identifiers: LCCN 2016054107 (print) | LCCN 2016056158 (ebook) |
  ISBN 9780778733713 (reinforced library binding : alk. paper) |
  ISBN 9780778733775 (pbk. : alk. paper) |
  ISBN 9781427119018 (Electronic HTML)
Subjects: LCSH: Levers--Juvenile literature. | Simple machines--Juvenile
  literature. | Makerspaces--Juvenile literature.
Classification: LCC TJ147 .M5377 2017 (print) | LCC TJ147 (ebook) |
  DDC 621.8/11--dc23
LC record available at https://lccn.loc.gov/2016054107

Crabtree Publishing Company

www.crabtreebooks.com   1-800-387-7650

Printed in Canada/032017/BF20170111

Published in Canada
Crabtree Publishing
616 Welland Ave.
St. Catharines, Ontario
L2M 5V6

Published in the United States
Crabtree Publishing
PMB 59051
350 Fifth Avenue, 59th Floor
New York, New York 10118

Published in the United Kingdom
Crabtree Publishing
Maritime House
Basin Road North, Hove
BN41 1WR

Published in Australia
Crabtree Publishing
3 Charles Street
Coburg North
VIC 3058

CONTENTS

YOU CAN BE A MAKER!

Makers are people who find new ways to solve problems and do tasks. They experiment and learn in a hands-on way. Makers also dream up ways to reuse everyday items. Are you ready to be a maker? From catapults to pinball movers, the projects in this book will help get you started!

TEAMWORK

Makers often team up to share their skills and supplies. Working together with other makers also leads to more ideas and points of view. You can learn a lot from the ideas of others! **Makerspaces** are places where makers work together. You could visit makerspaces in your school or library, or set up your own makerspace and invite some friends to join you!

A new way of learning

There is no right or wrong way to make something.
Makers know that:

✓ The only limit is your imagination.

✓ Every idea or question—even ones that seem silly—
could lead to something amazing.

✓ Each team member adds value to a project.

✓ Things do not always go as planned. This is part of being a maker!
Challenges help us think creatively.

WHAT IS A LEVER?

What do scissors, nutcrackers, and hand brakes on bikes have in common? They all use levers! A lever is a simple machine. These machines are tools with few or no moving parts. They change the amount or direction of a force. Force is the effort needed to push or pull on an object.

PARTS OF A LEVER

A lever has a stiff, movable arm or bar. Part of the arm connects to a fixed turning point called a **fulcrum**. The arm **pivots**, or turns, on the fulcrum. This is why a fulcrum is sometimes called a pivot.

HELP WITH WORK

Levers can make **work** easier, faster, or safer. Work is the use of force to move an object from one place to another. Using a lever makes it less work to lift or move objects. For example, the claw part of a hammer is a lever. It makes it easier and faster to pull up nails from floors or walls. The place where the claw meets the rest of the hammer is the fulcrum. The claw part is the lever's arm.

arm

fulcrum

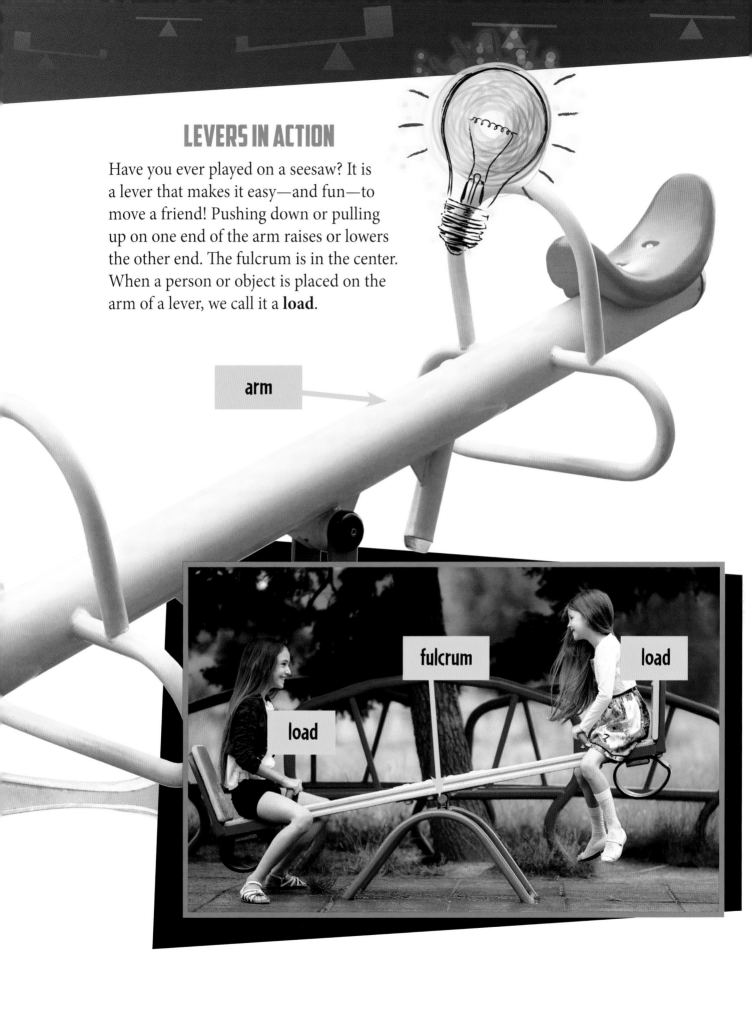

LEVERS IN ACTION

Have you ever played on a seesaw? It is a lever that makes it easy—and fun—to move a friend! Pushing down or pulling up on one end of the arm raises or lowers the other end. The fulcrum is in the center. When a person or object is placed on the arm of a lever, we call it a **load**.

arm

load

fulcrum

load

MAKE A LEVER

Building a lever will help you understand its parts and function, or use, better. By changing the setup of the lever, you will discover how the distance between the fulcrum and the load affects the amount of force needed to lift the load and the distance it can be lifted. This will help you with the maker missions in this book.

SET IT UP!

1. Tape the toilet paper roll to the table. This is the fulcrum.

2. Make a loop of tape and attach it to one end of the ruler. The ruler is the arm.

3. Place the arm across the fulcrum as shown. The center of the arm should rest on the fulcrum.

Materials

- Ruler
- Toilet paper roll or a spool of thread to act as the fulcrum
- Masking tape
- A small beanbag, eraser, or an object of similar weight to act as the load

Setup #1

load

arm

force

fulcrum

4. Press the beanbag onto the tape to secure it to the arm.

5. Lift the load by pressing down on the opposite end of the arm.

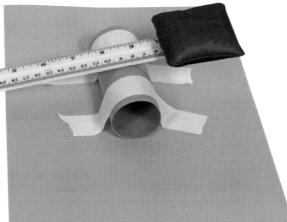

6. Reposition the arm so the load is as close to the fulcrum as possible. Press down on the opposite end of the arm to lift the load.

Setup #3

7. Reposition the arm so the load is as far away from the fulcrum as possible. Lift the load by pressing down on the opposite end of the arm.

Once you understand how a simple machine works, you will be able to modify, or change, it to solve different problems. How you build each lever will change based on the criteria of each maker mission. For example, the materials or position of the fulcrum may change from challenge to challenge. Check out the "Modify Your Machine" boxes throughout the book.

Think About It

Which lever setup made it easiest to lift the load?

Which was more difficult?

Which lever setup lifted the load the highest?

Are you ready to get creative with levers? Start each of the maker projects in this book by brainstorming. Take five minutes to come up with as many ideas as possible. No idea is too out there! Write them on chart paper or sticky notes. If you work with a group, respect other people's ideas.

Choose an idea from your list and make a plan. When you have a plan, draw it and measure each part of your project carefully. Remember to be open-minded. Where your project starts may not be where it ends up!

Helpful hints

Running into problems is part of the maker process. If you are stuck, try some of the following tips:

- Think about solutions to problems or challenges you have solved in the past. There may be some parts you could add to or change to help you solve this problem or challenge.

- Break up the problem or challenge into small parts and focus on solving one part at a time.

- State how you will know if you have solved the problem or challenge. Fill in the blank: I will know I have solved the problem when _____.

- Look at your list of ideas. **Ask:** Can we combine two or more ideas into one?

- Think about each part of your problem or challenge. **Ask:** Is there a certain part or area that is not working?

LEVERS THAT RAISE

Simple machines can pack a lot of power! Have you ever tried to move a large, heavy rock? Using a lever would have been helpful. These tools can make it easier and safer to lift a heavy load.

LIFTING LEVERS

To move a big rock, you could use a long wooden board. This style of lever arm helps people move loads that are too heavy to lift. One end of the board wedges as far under the rock as it can go. A fulcrum, such as a smaller rock, rests on the ground beneath the board. Pushing down on the other end of the board lifts the load!

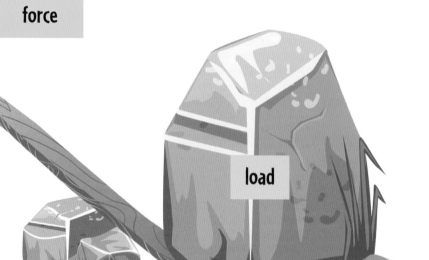

force

load

fulcrum

load

distance

fulcrum

PIVOT POWER

Lifting a load is easier when the fulcrum is close to it. The closer the fulcrum is to the load, the less force is needed to move it. The distance also affects how high the load lifts. The load goes higher when the fulcrum is placed away from it.

force

TRY IT!

It is easy to make your own lever that lifts a load. Get started with the challenge on the next page. Be sure to start with brainstorming. Choose your best idea and remember to sketch out all your plans.

MAKE IT LIFT

Get ready to do some heavy lifting! Make a lever to lift a load that is at least five pounds (2.27 kg). Your lever must lift the load at least 1 inch (2.54 cm) off the ground.

Materials

- Paper
- Pencil
- Arm, such as a long wooden board
- Fulcrum, such as a thick book
- Load, such as a loaded backpack or sack of flour

MODIFY YOUR MACHINE

Make sure that the arm of your lever is firm and strong. Picture the example of the long wooden board on pages 12-13.

THINK ABOUT IT

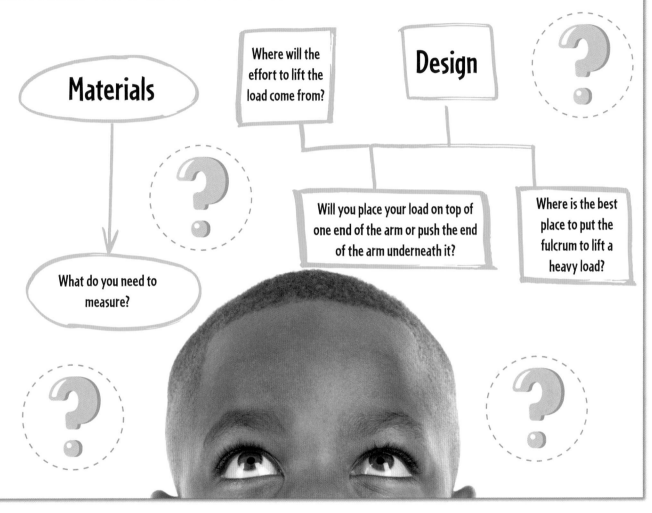

Materials

Where will the effort to lift the load come from?

Design

?

?

What do you need to measure?

Will you place your load on top of one end of the arm or push the end of the arm underneath it?

Where is the best place to put the fulcrum to lift a heavy load?

?

?

MISSION ACCOMPLISHED

Test your lever. Did you lift your load as described in the Maker Mission? If not, what could you try next?

If your lever worked as planned, flip to page 30 for more ideas to try with it.

LEVERS THAT MOVE

Some levers help do the work of moving objects inside closed-off spaces. Have you ever seen a pinball machine in an arcade? Among the flashing lights and fun sounds, levers are hard at work to help players score big!

INSIDE THE MACHINE

Glass tops allow people to see inside pinball machines. They also stop players from reaching into them to touch the parts or move the ball. Instead, users push buttons that are connected to levers. The levers do the work of moving the pinball around the machine.

HOW DOES IT WORK?

The fulcrum on a pinball machine lever is at one end of its arm. The arm pivots when the user pushes a button. The force of the arm hitting the pinball sends it shooting away. The direction and speed of the pinball depends on where it makes contact with the lever.

TRY IT!

Do you want to make your own pinball-style lever? Check out the Make it Roll challenge on the next page. Build on the ideas there and use your imagination to come up with something fun with your friends!

MAKE IT ROLL

Are you ready to roll? Make a lever to move a small, rolling object such as a ball or a marble. The object must travel a distance of at least 3 feet (91 cm).

Materials

- Paper
- Pencil
- Measuring tape or ruler
- Arm
- Fulcrum, such as a pencil on which the arm can pivot
- Small ball or marble

MODIFY YOUR MACHINE

You will need a firm material to use for the arm. The fulcrum may need to attach to the arm.

THINK ABOUT IT

Materials

Would it be helpful to create some kind of frame with cardboard or wood to keep the ball in an enclosed area?

Will this project work better with the arm placed flat or on its side?

Design

Where is the best place to put the fulcrum? Should it be under the arm or along its side? How will the arm pivot on the fulcrum?

How will the ball make contact with the arm? Will you roll it toward the arm or start with it resting against the arm?

MISSION ACCOMPLISHED

Test your lever in an open space on the ground. Note your results. Did your object roll at least 3 feet (91 cm)? If not, what could you try next?

If your project was a success, find ideas to mix it up on page 30.

LEVERS THAT LAUNCH

Get ready to meet another kind of lever that moves loads like no other machine does. When the arm of a catapult pivots, it hurls objects through the air at high speed. It makes the work of moving objects fast and easy.

CATAPULT ARM

There are many kinds of catapults. One of the most basic styles looks a lot like a seesaw. The arm is usually long and narrow.

Many catapults have a cuplike holder at one end of the arm. The load goes into the holder so it will not fall off the arm.

HOW DOES IT WORK?

To make an object fly far and fast, the effort is placed on the opposite end to the load. The more effort placed on the load, the farther it will fly! Moving the fulcrum away from the load also increases the height it will fly. Another way to do this is to make the arm longer or the fulcrum higher. These changes cause the lever to move farther in the air.

TRY IT!

Make your own catapult to see how this kind of lever works. Remember that makers often work in teams. Sharing ideas and materials will help you make a better catapult. Get started on the next page!

MAKE IT FLY

MAKER MISSION

It is time to fly high! Make a catapult to hurl an object through the air. Your lever must move a load at least 2 feet (61 cm) away. Make sure that you are in a safe, open place when you test your catapult. Do not choose an object with hazards such as sharp edges that could hurt someone.

Materials

- Paper
- Pencil
- Measuring tape or ruler
- Arm, such as a ruler or craft stick
- Fulcrum, such as multiple erasers that can be stacked to the desired height
- Load, such as cotton balls or craft pom-poms (try to choose soft and light objects for safety)
- Holder, such as a single-serve yogurt tub
- Tape, glue, or other materials to attach your containers to the arm

MODIFY YOUR MACHINE

You may need a stronger material to fasten the load's holder to the arm. The lever will need to be bigger and stronger than the one you built on pages 8-9.

THINK ABOUT IT

Materials

Size

Design

How can you adjust the fulcrum's height?

How will you choose the container that will hold the load?

Where will you place the fulcrum to make the load fly at least 2 feet (61 cm) away?

How will you add effort to one end of the lever to make it work?

How will you attach it to the catapult's arm?

MISSION ACCOMPLISHED

Make sure to clear an area before testing your catapult! Measure to see if you met the mission goals. If your lever did not work as you expected it to, what could you try next?

Once your catapult works well, try the Endless Ideas on page 30.

LEVERS THAT MEASURE

Levers are very old simple machines. People in Egypt found one clever use for levers over 7,000 years ago! They figured out how to use a lever to compare the weights of two different loads.

BALANCING ACT

Have you ever seen a balancing scale? Two containers of equal size and shape attach to either end of the arm. They may be hanging baskets or shallow bowls. They hold the loads so they do not fall off the arm. The arm must pivot freely on the fulcrum.

HOW DOES IT WORK?

To understand how a balancing scale works, picture a seesaw. The fulcrum in the middle helps balance the loads of the two riders. What happens when one seesaw rider is heavier than the other rider is? When the arm pivots, the heavier person lowers to the ground and the lighter one rises in the air! Scales work in the same way. It is easy to see which load is heavier because it lowers the arm.

TRY IT!

Flip the page to get started on your own scale. Remember that makers never give up. Keep trying and you will end up with something awesome!

MAKE IT BALANCE

Try out your maker skills by creating your own balancing scale. Your lever must balance two different loads of exactly the same weight. Experiment with measuring the number of the different objects needed to have equal weights. For example, how many marbles might equal 100 popcorn kernels?

Materials

- Paper
- Pencil
- Arm, such as a ruler
- Fulcrum, such as a triangular block
- Loads to compare, such as marbles and popcorn kernels or rocks and grains of rice
- 2 containers, such as small yogurt containers
- Tape, glue, or other materials to attach your containers to the arm

MODIFY YOUR MACHINE

You will need to choose a fulcrum made of a strong material that has a pointed or rounded top, so that the arm can balance correctly.

26

THINK ABOUT IT

Size

Design

How will the height of the fulcrum make a difference to your design?

If the containers on each end of the bar are not exactly the same, how will that affect your project?

What happens if the fulcrum is not at the very center of the arm?

How will you know if your loads are exactly the same weight?

How will the arm of your lever pivot on the fulcrum?

MISSION ACCOMPLISHED

Test your scale and make notes about anything you need to change. Did your lever balance out? Once it works well, try something new with it!

Find some ideas on page 30.

MORE MACHINES

There are five other kinds of simple machines. Have you ever seen the examples below making work easier, safer, or faster?

NAME	PURPOSE	PICTURE	EXAMPLES
inclined planes	move objects between two heights		water slide funnel wheelchair ramp
pulleys	lift, lower, or move objects; transfer force from one object to another		flagpole zip line bicycle chain
screws	join, cut into, lift, or lower objects		jar and lid drill light bulb
wedges	split apart or lift objects; stop objects from moving		ax door stop shovel
wheels and axles	move objects		Ferris wheel rolling pin skateboard

COMPLEX MACHINES

Joining two or more simple machines creates a **complex machine**. A wheelbarrow is an example of a complex machine. The handles and bin combine to form a lever. The wheel and axle is the fulcrum. They also make it easier and faster to push a heavy load over a surface.

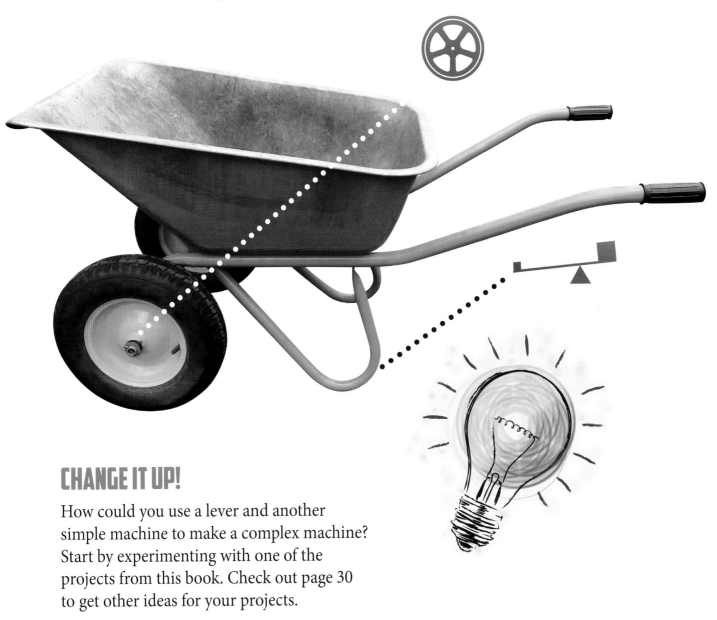

CHANGE IT UP!

How could you use a lever and another simple machine to make a complex machine? Start by experimenting with one of the projects from this book. Check out page 30 to get other ideas for your projects.

ENDLESS IDEAS

Experiment by adding other simple machines to your projects. You could also try some of the ideas listed below!

Make It Lift (pages 14–15):

- What changes could you make to lift a load that is twice as heavy?
- What materials did you use to create a strong lifting lever?
- Test some other materials and see how they work.

Make It Roll (pages 18–19):

- How could you make a variety of pinball levers that work together to move the ball along a set course?
- Think about the materials you might need to use. How will you stop the ball from flying away from the course? Try it with some friends!

Make It Fly (pages 22-23):

- Many catapults include elastic materials that provide extra force. For example, pulling down a lever's arm against an elastic band makes it fly forward with extra force when you let go. How could you modify your project by adding elastics to it?

Make It Balance (pages 26-27):

- Is there a different way that you could attach the lever to the fulcrum?
- Try placing your containers and loads in different positions along the arm. How does that change how the scale balances?

LEARNING MORE

BOOKS

Bailey, Gerry. *Pressing Down: The Lever.* Crabtree, 2014.

Howse, Jennifer. *Levers.* Weigl, 2014.

Oxlade, Chris. *Making Machines with Levers.* Raintree, 2016.

Volpe, Karen. *Get to Know Levers.* Crabtree, 2009.

WEBSITES

Watch a video about levers at the PBS Kids website.

http://pbskids.org/designsquad/video/what-are-levers

Learn more about how the parts of a lever work together and then test your skills with an online game.

www.learn4good.com/games/physics/equilibrium.htm

Review lever basics and watch a short video to see levers in action at this website.

http://mocomi.com/lever

Try another lever challenge at the PBS Kids website.

http://pbskids.org/designsquad/parentseducators/resources/pop_fly.html

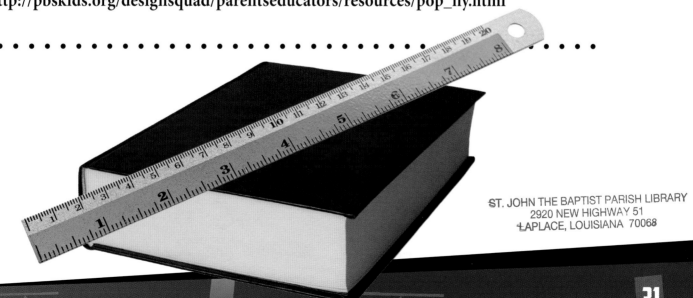

GLOSSARY

arcade A place where people play a variety of games, such as pinball or video games

brainstorming Coming up with as many ideas as possible to solve a problem or answer a question

complex machine A machine that combines at least two simple machines

effort The amount of energy, or power, used to do something

force The effort needed to push or pull on an object

fulcrum The fixed, or unmoving, turning point of a lever

lever A simple machine in which an arm turns on a fulcrum

load An object or person placed on the arm of a lever

makerspace A place where makers work together and share their ideas and resources

pivot The action of turning

simple machine A tool with few or no moving parts that people use to change the amount or direction of a force

work The use of force to move an object from one place to another

INDEX

ABOUT THE AUTHORS

Tim Miller is a mechanical engineer who loves to work with his hands. He is also a founding board member of Fusion Labworks, a maker community. Rebecca Sjonger is the author of over 40 children's books, including three titles in the *Be a Maker!* series.